Distributism Basics
An Explanation

David W. Cooney

Practical Distributism

Table of Contents

A Brief Introduction..1
Distributism vs. Socialism..4
Distributism vs. Christian Socialism..7
Distributism vs. Capitalism...12
The Science of Economics...19
The Nature and Roles of Government...23
Distributist Economic Society...28

A Brief Introduction

For those people who have just heard about distributism, whether they are just curious, or doubtful, I would like to present a few articles that run through the basics in simple terms. I'd like to be able to answer some of the claims presented by our detractors, but those answers must be understood by what distributism actually is, rather than what our detractors claim it to be.

Distributism, like capitalism and socialism, is the embodiment of certain views about how economic and political structures should work within a society. It has at times been called the "Third Way" of economics and also a "middle ground" between capitalism and socialism. It is true that distributism is a different way than either capitalism or socialism, but I disagree that it stands in between the two as if it takes parts of both or tries to blend them together. In fact, a better description of the differences would place distributism on one side, and both capitalism and socialism on the other. I hope this series will help you to see how that is.

Part of the confusion that leads people to think distributism somehow tries to negotiate a middle ground between capitalism and socialism is that we make some of the same arguments against both systems. We believe in limited government and the private ownership of property, but we also believe that the government does have a role in assisting society and that the concentration of large amounts of productive property in the hands of a few private owners leads to the the exploitation of the working classes. It is understandable that, without further investigation into how we think these problems should be remedied, people would conclude that we are somewhere in between the capitalist and socialist position. I hope in this series to present a clear, easy to understand, explanation of both where we stand and how our views are very different from both capitalism and socialism.

To begin to understand distributism, we must look at the founding of the movement. In 1891, Laissez Faire capitalism had been the predominant economic model in the West for some time. Laissez Faire is a view that government should not interfere in economics, or the businesses that make the economy work, except as needed to protect property rights and the peace of society. This led to wide masses of people being impoverished by extremely low wage jobs while a few were able to become extremely wealthy. This situation led to such great dissatisfaction in Western societies as a whole, that socialism actually looked good to people. In response to this threat, Pope Leo XIII wrote an encyclical called *Rerum Novarum*.

Rerum Novarum did not offer a new economic system. It outlined problems with capitalism as it was being practiced, and with the proposals of socialism. It urged that these problems be addressed, and presented the principles that should guide how to address them. It should be noted that, while the principles outlined were in keeping with the Gospel message, one should not expect otherwise from a pope, the philosophical view that served as the foundation was not exclusively Christian in nature.

In response to this call to resolve the problems evident in the Laissez Faire capitalism, and hoping to convince people who were considering socialism to consider another alternative, a group of Englishmen, led by G. K. Chesterton and Hilaire Belloc, started the distributist movement. In formulating their ideas, they looked to history to see where the injustices of the prevailing capitalist system crept in. They also looked further to see what was being done to avoid those injustices before then.

Distributists were not alone in the effort to address the problems of Laissez Faire capitalism. The socialist movement of the time was an effort to do the same. Even within the realm of capitalists, there were those who thought things needed to change. A capitalist economist named John Maynard Keynes sought to address the problems by altering the capitalist system itself. Keynes proposed more government intervention in economic and social matters while leaving the concentration of productive capital in place. To alleviate the impoverished state of the working classes, the government would tax the wealthy to fund programs to support the workers.

In the end, most countries adopted the modified version of capitalism proposed by Keynes and some adopted socialism. I will discuss some specifics about these in subsequent articles. Although the Keynesian system seemed to address the problems of Laissez Faire capitalism, in truth, it only worked by keeping the fundamentally unjust elements of that system in place. This prompted Pope Pius XI to write Quadragesimo Anno in 1931. Quadragesimo Anno was a follow-up to Rerum Novarum in which Pius XI discussed in greater detail why these systems are fundamentally flawed as solutions to the original problems addressed by Leo XIII.

Various forms of capitalism and socialism have been attempted in the last century, and they have all repeatedly failed. Many people are wondering what else can be done. The proposals of the distributists have been disregarded by professional and academic economists, leaving the average citizen unaware that they even existed. Many people are increasingly despairing of the possibility of finding a real solution to our economic and political problems because it seems to them that all of the options have been tried.

In the last several decades, the involvement of government in economics has expanded exponentially as more and more government programs to support the working classes and the poor have been implemented. The modern Libertarian economists (primarily of the "Austrian school") are loudly calling for a return to an essentially Laissez Faire model. They claim that we are on the road to all-out socialism. There is some justification to this because certain political and economic leaders seem to be advocating things very close to it.

Is this the moment for the distributist movement? Are the citizens of the Western world fed up with their "expert" economic leaders enough to consider trying a real alternative? Only time will tell.

Distributism vs. Socialism

In the late 19th and early 20th Centuries, three alternatives were proposed to alleviate the conditions of the working classes under capitalism: distributism, Keynesian capitalism, and socialism. Distributists are sometimes accused of being socialists, or at least quasi-socialists. This article will examine the nature of socialism and how it is completely incompatible with distributism.

Capitalism enabled the owners of corporations to greatly increase their wealth and eliminate any effective competition, making the vast majority of the working classes completely dependent on them. While the owners of these companies lived in luxury, the working class was reduced to a state where even having both parents work did not yield enough income to support a family. The lack of effective competition meant that workers could not simply leave their jobs for a better opportunity – better jobs didn't exist. The workers had to put up with whatever the employers wanted to make them endure, or they would be fired and be quickly replaced by others desperate for any work. It is no wonder that the promises of socialism appealed to many of them.

There are three basic fundamentals to the original idea of socialism, the first is the complete elimination of social classes, the second is the elimination of money, and the third is the elimination of a government run state. From the socialist view, the private ownership of property is what enables the classes to exist. The existence of a private claim to productive property enables some to elevate themselves above others, subjugating the workers to their ends and using their wealth to twist the powers of government to their advantage. Eliminating a private claim to productive property will enable the laborer to claim the benefit of his labor. Those in need will work according to their ability for the good of society – which means that each member of society will be guaranteed the fulfillment of his needs. This means that there is no need for money, which is merely a tool to transfer the private ownership of property. Since each person will act for the good of the whole society, and will do so voluntarily, there will be no need for government.

This original idea became known as *utopian socialism*. It was quickly supplanted with the idea of a "vanguard party" which, acting on behalf of the people, would secure the powers of the state. This vanguard party would implement "state capitalism" (also known as "state socialism") where the state would manage industry in much the same way as the capitalist did, but of course for the benefit of the society. This new form of socialism became known as *scientific socialism*.

4

Scientific socialism is the form of socialism of societies like the former Soviet Union and present day China. While it is true that there are various strains of socialist thought, this is the main embodiment of socialism as it has actually been implemented in any significant way. While the original utopian socialism would eliminate all private property, many socialist societies allowed some degree of private property which operated at the sufferance of, and sometimes under the direction of the state. While utopian socialism would eliminate all classes, all socialist societies actually replaced the old set of leaders with their own, and transferred the control of the majority of productive property from the hands of the few capitalists into the hands of the few political leaders. While utopian socialism would eliminate the state altogether, the existence of other states necessitated the continued existence of a state government with a capable military.

This last point is very important to understand about socialism. It cannot coexist with other "countries" except in isolation from them. The utopian version of a stateless socialism means that there cannot be a threat from outside of its society. Within its society, everyone is supposed to act according to the needs of society as a whole – they will do this voluntarily. In the socialist view, however, the existence of private property causes the greed and strife that lead to wars of conquest and the impoverishing of the masses. Therefore, a stateless socialist society cannot truly coexist with a capitalist society because the greed and strife of the latter will "obviously" lead it to attack the Utopia of the purely socialist society. While I think there is even a degree to which multiple socialist societies could not coexist, the attempt to create a truly socialist society necessitates either complete economic and military isolation from any capitalist societies, or the elimination of those societies altogether. I am not saying this is something they declared; it is merely the reality.

Unlike socialists, distributists do not consider the existence of privately owned property to be the problem with capitalism. As G. K. Chesterton quipped, *"the problem with capitalism is not that there are too many capitalists, but that there are too few."* The problem is that capitalism allows the ownership of the majority of productive property to become concentrated into the hands of a small minority of the population. The rest must become workers completely dependent on that minority for a wage on which to live.

Instead of seeking the socialist solution of eliminating private property by transferring the ownership of it into the hands of state controllers, distributism proposes the widest possible private ownership of property that can be achieved in a practical way. Unlike utopian socialists, distributists do not expect to establish a perfect society in which all of the people consistently voluntarily act for the good of society as a whole. In other words, distributism does not advocate the stateless society. Unlike the scientific socialists, distributists to not believe in empowering the state to manage potentially all economic activity for the good of the society. Distributism proposes a society structured on the principles of subsidiarity, where the lower foundational levels of society have natural rights which the higher levels cannot usurp. Even when assisting those lower levels, the higher levels cannot usurp the roles and functions which rightfully belong to the lower levels.

As you can see, the form of economic and political society proposed by distributism is fundamentally different than that proposed by socialism. Yes, distributists criticize the instability and injustices of the capitalist system as do the socialists, but the solutions proposed by the distributists are completely incompatible with the solutions proposed by socialism. Indeed, from the distributist perspective, the solutions proposed by socialism are in ways more unjust than the problems of capitalism they propose to solve.

Distributism vs. Christian Socialism

One reaction to this *Distributism Basics* series is that a particular group of commenters has asserted that their economic and political theories are so close to distributism as to make them virtually indistinguishable. In various ways, they have assured me that, if I would only read the writings explaining their views, I would be left scratching my head wondering what separates them from my own. Is this true? Is distributism just another name for what others call "Christian socialism?"

Because this assertion is that distributism and Christian socialism are essentially the same, I've decided that this specific claim needs to be addressed as an addition to the more general explanation of the incompatibility of distributism and socialism I previously published. Therefore, even though this article has been written after the rest of this series, I am inserting it after the previous article on socialism, and it should be considered the third in the series.

The purpose of this article is two-fold: On the one hand, it is to explain to Christian socialists the reasons why their view is fundamentally at odds with distributism. On the other hand, I hope to show any other readers who suspect that distributism must be some form of socialism why that is absolutely not the case. As I pointed out in the first article of this series, distributists make many of the same criticisms against capitalism as the socialists, but we also make many of the same criticisms against socialism as the capitalists. Christian socialism is no exception to that assertion, despite the claims of certain Christian socialists that their views are the same as those of distributists.

The apparent confusion on this point lies in how close their view appears to be to distributism. This is not as much in the fact that we make the same criticisms of capitalism, but because the terms some of them use when advocating their positions are very similar to those used by distributists. However, this similarity is only on the surface. It is said that the devil is in the details, and it is precisely in the details where the irreconcilable differences between distributism and Christian socialism can be seen as if in a bright light.

For this article, I have reviewed three writings by authors recommended to me by Christian socialists: *The Acquisitive Society* by R. H. Tawney, *Progress and Poverty* by Henry George, and *The Great Transformation* by Karl Polanyi. While I believe these authors were sincere in their attempt to address the injustices capitalists seemed incapable or unwilling to address through capitalism, and I believe many of their criticisms of capitalism were both just and correct, they seemed to miss where their proposed solutions were just as faulty as the other socialists they criticized. Ultimately, the views Christian socialists have about the nature of property and economics, the relationship of those things to the individual and society, and the relationship of society to the individual, is no less utilitarian and materialistic than those of any other form of socialism. While the end goals of the Christian socialists and distributists may sound similar, the basis for justifying both those goals and the methods proposed for accomplishing them are incompatible.

While Christian socialists appear to agree with distributists that there is no such thing as an absolute right to an unregulated use of private property, they appear to disagree that the right to own and pass on to heirs property legally obtained, including property in land, is inviolable. Distributsts advocate policies that promote the widest practical ownership of productive property, but they must be formulated to avoid injustice against current owners. They must encourage as natural a transition from concentrated to distributed ownership as possible. The idea of merely abolishing title by a stroke of law, as suggested by some of these authors, is not compatible with distributism. In addition, the position of the Christian socialists seems to put the power of regulation in the highest levels of the government, but distributists insist that it must be local wherever possible and practical.

R. H. Tawney asserted that he would apparently deprive ownership to those who own property for rent in urban areas but not those in rural areas. He also asserted that the state should invest in and maintain ownership of large industries and advocated a form of joint ownership between the state and the workers. This is not presented as a temporary measure. He wrote that the state should acquire title (either exclusive or joint) to productive property and hold it. Many of his other views are not necessarily incompatible with distributism, but his views on the rights of property ownership are not in line with the other writers suggested to me. In my view, this makes his association with Christian socialism tenuous at best. However, his views on joint state and private ownership appear to have gone beyond public ownership of resources and utilities. Based on this, it seems to me that he may have been more of a corporatist than a distributist.

As we move on to Henry George, it must be remembered that distributism is not an attempt to negotiate a middle ground between capitalism and socialism. It does not attempt a harmonious blending of the two. Mr. George, on the other hand, declared this was his specific intention. He asserted that you may own your house, your shop and all the things in them, but not the land on which they sit or any natural resources of that land. Distributists advocate as many people as possible, or at least as practical, to privately own productive property, including land.

Mr. George also accepted usurious forms of interest charged on loans of money, justifying it on the grounds that, because the activities of production result in a general increase throughout society, and even throughout the world, the charging of interest on money loaned achieves an overall economic balance. The problem with this justification is that the lender is effectively protected from loss while the borrower is not. The chance of the borrower getting an increase is tied to the success of his activity, but the lender's chance of increase is tied to the presumption of overall increase rather than his ability to wisely choose borrowers. Not only is usury not compatible with distributism, the idea of a transaction where only one side holds a risk is fundamentally unjust. What Mr. George advocated is a scheme where the borrower is at risk based on his particular endeavor, but the lender is guaranteed an increase based on the presumption of an average general increase of all endeavors including those with which he has no involvement. In other words, if I make a business loan to you, and your business fails, you lose but I still win.

Exactly how Karl Polanyi's, *The Great Transformation*, could be presented as evidence that Christian socialism is essentially the same as distributism remains beyond my comprehension. While he seemed willing to apply some level of subsidiarity to national government, this was only for the purpose of preserving culture. I found no evidence that his idea of subsidiarity really applied to anything else, or that it applied for anything more local than the state. He dismissed subsidiarity altogether in economic matters. This is because, in his view, industrialized economy has moved beyond national boundaries, making those boundaries anachronistic for modern economics. I have not found this notion in any explanation of distributism. Even though this is enough to show that Polanyi's views are not compatible, there is another point where he clearly diverges from distributism.

As I explained in my article, *Is Distributism Catholic?*, the philosophical basis for many distributist positions predate Christianity. Additionally, you can find teachings very close to distributism in many other faiths. The distributist movement has basically always had adherents who are not Catholic, and even some who are not Christian, but while these could typically assert the compatibility of distributism with their own faiths, I don't believe any of them would have denied its origins, much less its compatibility with the Christian Gospels. As I explained in the first article of this series, distributism, as a distinct and named economic system, was founded by Catholics in response to papal teaching. I don't think that anyone who has studied distributism, even if they disagree with it, would deny that its positions are an attempt to apply philosophical positions on economic and social structures in ways that are specifically compatible with the Catholic Faith.

Some Christian socialists who have assured me that their views are nearly exactly the same as distributism have directed me to Mr. Polanyi's writings for evidence of this claim. Instead of evidence of an economic system based on the idea that the Gospel message still applies to modern societies, Mr. Polanyi rejects this idea, agreeing instead with Robert Owen's assertion that *"the Gospels ignored the reality of society."*

"Owen recognized that the freedom we gained through the teachings of Jesus was inapplicable to a complex society. His socialism was the upholding of man's claim to freedom in such a society. The post-Christian era of Western civilization had begun, in which the Gospels did not any more suffice, and yet remained the basis of our civilization.

The discovery of society is thus either the end or rebirth of freedom. While the fascist resigns himself to relinquishing freedom and and glorifies power which is the reality of society, the socialist resigns himself to that reality and upholds the claim to freedom, in spite of it. Man becomes mature and able to exist as a human being in a complex society. To quote once more Robert Owen's inspired words: 'Should any causes of evil be irremovable by the new powers which men are about to acquire, they will know that they are necessary and unavoidable evils; and childish, unavailing complaints will cease to be made.'"

If this is a position of Christian socialism, in what way is it compatible with distributism? In what way can it maintain a claim to being Christian?

While some of the goals of Christian socialists sound similar to those of distributists, the underlying justifications Christian socialists give for their goals reveal a philosophical foundation that is at odds with that of distributism. These get mixed with other goals that are not in the least compatible so that, in the end, what Christian socialists wish to accomplish is not the same as distributists. Because of this, the results of implementing their overall goals will naturally be very different from the results of distributism. In addition, the methods condoned by Christian socialists to achieve their goals cannot be accepted by distributists. These authors, recommended to me by Christian socialists, have affirmed my conviction that pope Pius XI was correct when he wrote:

"If Socialism, like all errors, contains some truth (which, moreover, the Supreme Pontiffs have never denied), it is based nevertheless on a theory of human society peculiar to itself and irreconcilable with true Christianity. Religious socialism, Christian socialism, are contradictory terms; no one can be at the same time a good Catholic and a true socialist."

There is one final point I feel I need to address in this article. Distributists have been criticized by certain capitalists for not rejecting the notion of a progressive tax as an instrument to facilitate the transition from capitalism to distributism. Among these criticisms is the notion that, because socialists, like Marx, also supported progressive taxation, this proves we actually are socialists. Since this article, combined with the previous article in this series on socialism, addresses the fundamental incompatibility of distributism with socialism, I will take this opportunity to address this specific criticism on two points.

The first point is the idea that, because some socialists supported an idea, anyone else who supports that idea must also be socialist (no matter how forcefully they renounce socialism). Well, the socialists I reviewed for this article not only allow for, but actively advocate the private ownership of the tools of production. One advocated charging of interest on money loaned. If these capitalists are to be consistent, they must either reject the ideas of interest charged on money loaned and private ownership of the tools of production, or admit that they are really socialists. I am, of course, kidding, but this does illustrate that one has to look at the entire position presented and cannot justly accuse someone of being a socialist merely because of one or two particular points where their positions seem to match. Distributism, as a system, rejects fundamental principles that are the very root of socialism.

The second point is that, while I cannot speak for other distributists, I consider progressive taxation to be an extreme case solution. This is because, as I stated in previous writings and comments, there are certainly aspects of progressive taxation that can be considered unjust. It could only be considered if, after a true attempt to apply more just methods, they were found to be inadequate for accomplishing sufficient change. Even then, due consideration to the principle of double-effect would have to be applied. I would also point out that, in my view, progressive taxation would only really be compatible with distributism if done at a local level rather than at a state or federal level. I admit that, at this time, I believe that it is likely to be needed, but this is because capitalists have historically used taxes and other laws to establish the current economic environment, and those same tools may be needed to undo what they've set up. However, this is an issue I am still studying, so my position on this may change. Regardless, I would be happiest if the wider distribution of privately owned productive property could be accomplished without this type of drastic measure. I would strongly advocate avoiding progressive taxation if doing so is possible because I believe not using such measures is more consistent with the fundamental ideas behind distributism.

Distributism vs. Capitalism

"Distributism is just like capitalism, except that we differ on the nature of man, the purpose of economic activity, usury, the maximization of token wealth, the role and legitimate exercise of the state, empirical economics, the meaning of subsidiarity, subordination of economics to the higher sciences, our ends, our means, what money is, what wealth is, what a free market is, production and consumption, regulation, free trade, the moral and divine law in the social and economic order, and, yes, what liberty means."

- Richard Aleman

In order to discuss the differences between distributism and capitalism, we must first discuss what capitalism is. I know that many people assume they already know what capitalism is, but I contend that they are only partly correct in their knowledge. I think what they believe to be capitalism is part of it, but capitalism also includes specific things they might not consider as part of it, and with which they may actually disagree.

For many people, the idea of capitalism does not go much farther than the right to private property and free market competition. It is when you get into more specific details of these and other aspects of capitalism that the differences between what people think it is (or should be) and what it actually is come to light. Are there reasonable limits to the use of private property? Is a market truly free if monopolies exist? Should local government be able to prevent a store like Wal-Mart from opening in the community in order to preserve the existing local businesses? It is in the details where you can find great differences of opinion among self-professed capitalists.

Have we really considered what truly defines capitalism? What sets it apart from the economic systems that preceded it? What sets it apart from socialism? What sets it apart from distributism? Capitalism is that economic system where the private ownership of productive capital is separated from the work on that capital, and where the laws not only facilitate, but give advantage to that separation. Many will disagree with the last part of that definition, but the reality is that capitalism has never existed without the use of laws to give advantage to certain business interests. Whether we are discussing protectionist tariffs, or the seizure of the commons to give them to already wealthy merchant lords, or the forced disbanding of the guilds, the manipulation and use of the power of government has always been an integral part of capitalism.

We need to realize that there is no such thing as an economic society without political involvement in economics. Utopian socialism had to morph into scientific socialism. Even those capitalists who advocate a "minimalist" view of the role of government in economics promote whatever involvement they consider to be the most advantageous to businesses, whether it is the establishment of government protections in the form of patents or copyrights, or laws preventing fraud, or other government enforced protections. While distributism promotes subsidiarity, that really just keeps government involvement to as local a level as practical, based on our belief that this will best protect economic freedom by allowing local citizens to have a real and effective voice.

Just as we say that a society is socialist when a determining amount of its productive capital is legally barred from being privately owned, a society is capitalist when a determining amount of its productive capital is privately owned by people who do not do the work due to laws enabling and encouraging the separation of ownership and work. The "determining amount" is not a hard and fast rule. It is that amount which would generally be accepted as establishing the tone or mode of the society. The separation of private ownership from work is at the root of various aspects of capitalism: usury, free trade, the combative relationship between labor and owners, the stock market, the consolidation of wealth resulting in monopolies and the consequent anti-trust issues.

In his 1912 book, *The Servile State*, Hilaire Belloc wrote that capitalism was moving toward two inevitable ends which he termed the Servile State and the Distributive (or Proprietary) State. While scientific socialism is very close to what he described as a Servile State, Belloc didn't think it likely that societies would choose the socialist route because of the extreme disruption to economic life it entailed. While he may have been wrong about some societies being willing to try the socialist route, he was clearly correct about the economic disruption.

What Belloc considered more likely than the move toward socialism was modifications to capitalism which would preserve the essence of the prevailing capitalist structure - the majority of productive capital controlled by a minority of wealthy owners - but would implement government imposed protections against the economic injustices the workers were facing at the time. These protections for the workers were not without their own obligations, however, in order for the workers to get them they would be legally compelled to work for the owners. This is the essence of what he called the Servile State.

This legal requirement would not necessarily involve the government dictating where individual people would work. The workers may remain free to move from employer to employer in a Servile State, but the legal protections to provide the needs of the people, both while they worked and in times when they didn't, would be based on the obligation of the masses to work for the few owners of large concentrations of productive property. Even if small proprietors remained, the laws would favor the large proprietors, protecting the concentration of ownership. This would effectively compel large numbers of workers to work for the large proprietors. If this were done correctly, Belloc maintained, capitalism would become stable. The majority of the large proprietors would welcome the restrictions and obligations imposed on them because it would guarantee that they would maintain their wealth and status. The majority of the workers would welcome the obligation to work for the large proprietors because it came with promises that the deplorable conditions in which they lived would be greatly improved. Belloc stated that because capitalism had already concentrated so much wealth into the hands of a few large proprietors, society would find it much easier, much less disruptive to move toward a Servile State than either the Distributive State he advocated or the socialist collective state he did not.

In the same year that Belloc published The Servile State, John Maynard Keynes proposed a radical modification of the prevailing capitalist system which had resulted in the masses of workers living in poverty and wretched conditions. It is an unfortunate truth of capitalism that, because it tends to transfer wealth from the masses to the few proprietors, the workers - who are also the overwhelming majority of the customers - cease having enough money to buy. As the workers struggled just to have a place in which to live and food to eat, they necessarily stopped buying other things. To solve this situation, Keynes proposed a system where the government would tax the large proprietors to fund programs to assist the workers. The idea was that transferring enough wealth from the large proprietors back to the workers would relieve them of the worries of having to choose between the basic necessities of life and purchasing other products necessary to keep capitalism functioning. The result of these changes was that economic society became more stable, there were still disruptions, but they became less frequent. Belloc was at least partly correct in his predictions.

It needs to be understood that the Keynesian system is not a recipe for socialism. Both utopian and scientific socialism removed at least the vast majority of private ownership. Keynes' system not only maintains private ownership, but keeps it in the hands of the few large proprietors. In fact, the Keynesian plan is completely dependent on the continued existence of a very wealthy class of private owners. This is important to understand because some advocates of the Austrian School say that more government involvement in economics is actually socialism. In reality, the Keynesian plan was not one for the establishment of a socialist egalitarian society. The rhetoric behind all of these plans is nothing more than an extension of the Keynsian idea of transferring enough wealth from the haves to the have-nots because they believe that is what will keep the economy working.

The disagreement between the Austrians and the Keynesians ultimately boils down to the extent to which government should be involved in economic matters. The Austrians say they want government out of economics, but they really mean they only want government involved in ways they believe will protect and promote business interests. The Keynesians want government and business to work hand in hand, even if they are sometimes at odds over particular points, to try and maintain the maximization of corporate profit while not impoverishing the workers. The Austrians would argue that Keynesian economics is not capitalism because the government interferes in the free market. There is an element of truth to the argument. The Keynesian system is truly a movement away from capitalism to the Servile State. The question is whether the move has gone far enough at this point to say that we have truly moved from one to the other. The Servile State is neither capitalism nor socialism, but will ultimately result in a totalitarian plutocratic state just like socialism ultimately results in a totalitarian collectivist state. Capitalism on its own results in a plutocratic state that may not be totalitarian, but will be just as miserable for the majority of those who live in it.

Just as I don't believe Adam Smith envisioned the atrocities capitalism enabled, I don't think that Keynes necessarily envisioned everything that his system, under which we now live, has become, but Belloc did. What Keynes really accomplished, even if he didn't intend to do so, was a workable plan for the gradual and peaceful implementation of Belloc's Servile State. Today's advocates of the Austrian School are loudly calling for a return to the earlier, "truer," capitalism. We must ask, however, exactly how different is the current Austrian view from the policies of the 19th Century? Even if we disagree with what unions have become as political entities, have we forgotten why they were formed? Have we forgotten why the child labor laws had to be passed over the objections of big business?

Have we forgotten how difficult it was to actually get those laws passed due to the power that big business had over government? I don't claim that we would return immediately to the injustices of those days, but what does Austrian School propose that would prevent those types of things from eventually happening again? (And is that really consistent with what they call true capitalism?)

What, then, is the difference between capitalism and distributism? Capitalism is that economic system where the private ownership of productive capital is separated from the work on that capital. Distributism is that economic system where the private ownership of productive capital is joined to the work on that capital. When the determining amount of privately owned productive capital is worked on by the owners of that capital, the society is distributist.

This is where comparing distributism and capitalism can get confusing for some people. Capitalism does not reject the small proprietor who works on his own property. Capitalism does not reject worker-owned cooperatives. Therefore, the forms of businesses and ownership promoted by distributists are perfectly acceptable to capitalists. The difference is the acceptance by capitalists of the concentration of ownership into the hands of a few extremely wealthy owners. The difference is the foundational philosophical views that result in capitalists accepting, and distributist rejecting, things like usury, anti-competitive spending, monopoly, transactions where only one side is protected from risk, and the view that economics is a "natural" science like chemistry or physics to which things like ethics and justice don't necessarily apply.

It needs to be admitted that most people who consider themselves capitalists would argue that everyone should act in an ethical way in business as well as always. The point is that ethics has nothing to do with what capitalists say is the science of economics. The capitalist's idea of the science of economics would allow him to say, "It's not personal, it's business." The distributist's view of the science of economics would not allow him to say that. I'll write more about that in the next article of this series.

It is my opinion that the average person who considers himself a capitalist, the small proprietor, the typical employee, unknowingly agrees more with the economic views of distributism than the true nature of capitalism. They would rightly argue that capitalism can be ethical and just. What they don't realize is that there is nothing inherent in capitalism, nothing built into it at a philosophical level, to ensure or even promote ethical business practices. Sure there are laws against fraud and false advertising, but trying to otherwise ensure ethics in business is a separate issue that may (or may not) be applied by individual businessmen or corporations. In fact, ethics is only considered to be "good business sense" rather than part of the science of economics itself.

Another difference between capitalism and distributism is the ability for a community to influence and protect its local economy. In general, distributism accepts the idea that local businesses should be self-governing within guild structures. The structures need to be set up so that businesses are answerable to the local community they serve. Local communities can require local residency for running a business within its jurisdiction, but not be able to prevent tradesmen from bringing in goods produced in other areas. Capitalism rejects such things as interfering with what they call free market competition.

The capitalists idea of economics allows him to say that greed is good - not just bettering ones own position, but actively trying to *get all that he can for himself* (without fraud). Distributism has nothing against someone trying to better his own position, but still considers greed to be a vice. Distributism does not pretend to propose a system where there will be no wealthy and no poor. The idea is a Utopian absurdity. However, if the private ownership of productive property were wide spread, the disparity between the wealthy and middle classes, and between the middle and poor classes, would be less.

All of this is based on the idea that a great multitude of small, privately owned businesses is better for society, results in greater economic independence and freedom for the average citizen, than having large multi-national corporations employing tens of thousands of non-owner workers. The result of distributism will be more providers of all goods and services, which will increase employment options and better working conditions for workers, greater variety and more choice for customers, more acceptance by business of social responsibility to the community, and more stability in the local economy because more economic activity will circulate within a community rather than sending money out to distant corporate headquarters.

I agree with Belloc that moving to a distributist society involves a great change for that society. The social and economic changes would need to be worked out and implemented carefully because they are so radically different than what we currently have, so different than what we have been taught is the only just and workable system in the world. Beyond that, however, is the fact that distributism is based on a different philosophical view of economics than capitalism. For the distributist, economics is about families being able to provide for their needs and wants. This is the foundational principle that underlies everything else about economics, not the constant increase of the GDP, the price of shares on the stock exchanges, or being able to report record profits. The foundation of a healthy and stable national economy is for the various local economies to be healthy and stable. The collective resilience of local economies is a more accurate barometer of national economic health than the stock market.

The Science of Economics

There seems to be a theory, popular among the critics of distributism, that distributists either don't understand the science of economics, or that we don't believe economics is a science. To listen to them, we don't accept the laws of supply and demand, scarcity, the theory of diminishing returns, or the many other aspects of the science of economics. This, of course, is nonsense.

Let me perfectly clear. I don't deny that those things are part of economics. Where distributists disagree with our (typically capitalist) critics is in precisely what kind of science economics is, and how each of those aspects of economics is to be viewed in relation to other aspects. Why is it that, prior to the economic collapse in 2008, only a minority of the economists predicted the failure? In what other science could the "experts" get away with blaming others when their predictions go wrong while simultaneously declaring that their modeling was correct?

Science is the discipline of applying the principles of reason to evidence in order to reach a conclusion about the cause of the evidence observed. Even when engaging in theoretical fields of science, it is based on the evidence at hand. For any science to hope to be accurate and useful, it must deal with the matter at hand according to its nature. This, in my view, is where the "expert" economists go wrong. The reason I say they go wrong on this point is not because what they analyze in the field of economics is wrong, but because they don't include an important aspect of the nature of economics in their models. That aspect is people.

When I say this, I don't mean that they ignore people entirely in their economic models. If that were the case, advertising would not be a multi-billion dollar industry. However, advertisers know that different people respond to different advertising, and even with their extensive knowledge of behavior, they can make massive mistakes. Why then, do so many economic experts treat economics as though it were a speculative science, governed by rigid laws of nature like chemistry or physics?

Speculate means to look. The conclusions of the speculative sciences are based on seeing the object being studied. This "seeing" can be any reliable form of observation. Even the study of human nature (philosophical psychology) is a speculative science. The speculative sciences are for the sake of knowledge, and the conclusions we get from them are information. The practical sciences, on the other hand, are for the sake of doing. The conclusions of the practical sciences are about how to apply the knowledge we've learned from the speculative sciences. It is one thing to know the physics of an arch, but knowing how best to incorporate an arch into a building is a different kind of thing. It is possible to put an arch in a building so that the arch is working perfectly, but its location ruins the intended function of the building.

The principle function of economics is to provide for the needs and wants of the family through relational transactions with others. While economics involves material needs, it is the relational transactions used to get them that are the focus of the study of economics. Economics is a human activity that involves a relationship between people, so its principle factor is human nature. The law of supply and demand and the other factors that economists regularly study are part of economics. They are factors that affect the transactions, but economics is about the transactions themselves, and the transactions are relationships. Therefore the subject of economics is the *relationship* of humans involved in transactions. Economics is a science, but it is a practical science.

Because economics is about a type of relationship between humans, its conclusions must be based on and be consistent with human nature. Economics, therefore, is about how people should behave toward one another when engaged in transactions, no matter how trivial, to provide for their needs and wants. This applies to both sides of any economic transactions, because both the buyer and seller engage in these transactions to provide for their needs and wants. In other words, economics is about ethics, which is the serious and scientific study of acting in accordance with human nature.

Great things can be done when the relationship between the speculative and practical sciences is understood and respected. The speculative sciences gave us all the information needed to reach the moon, the practical sciences actually reached it. When dealing with the speculative sciences, consistent results allow us to predict outcomes. However, the conclusions of the practical sciences are not of the same kind as those of the speculative sciences. We can predict with reasonable reliability what will happen when mixing two chemicals under certain conditions because we have observed consistent results when those chemicals were mixed in those conditions in the past. The practical sciences are about what ought to be done, they are about how to apply the information we learned from the speculative sciences.

A financial deal that looks great on paper may get rejected because of a personal disagreement, prejudice, because one side thinks the deal is immoral, or just because one side wants to hold out for something better. On the other hand, some deals may be taken simply because they will yield a large return regardless of other factors. All of these decisions are economic decisions, but they are based on things that go beyond what economists say is part of the true science of economics. Because of this, economists cannot predict - they are

20

really incapable of predicting - something like a football player walking away from a promising career, being unwilling even to hold out to be vested in the NFL's pension plan. These actions don't fit in their models, but this choice is an economic decision by that player.

While most economists will proclaim that everyone should be ethical in their economic dealings, they still deny that ethics is part of the science of economics. In a way they are correct. Ethics is not part of the science of economics, economics is part of the science of ethics. Economics cannot be separated from ethics because it is a sub-field of ethics. Being ethical in your economic activity is not simply "good business sense," it is an essential and inseparable element of any and all economic activity. This is why the phrase, "it's not personal, it's business," is incompatible with distributism. Economics is a human action that takes place in a relationship between people. It can't be anything but personal.

Distributists don't claim that the failure of economists to accurately predict economic outcomes is because economics is not a science, but because it is a different kind of science than economists believe it to be. Their models fail because they look at people as economic numbers, or more likely because they look at economic numbers without adequately considering the relationship of those numbers to actual people who are more worried about the immediate issues of providing for their families than how a multi-billion dollar company is doing on the stock market. I believe this is why the recent efforts to fix the economy have failed. They gave trillions of dollars to the biggest banks so that they would start lending. They not only failed to see that the people were unwilling to go further into debt, they then blamed those people for the continued failure of the economic recovery. I ask again, in what other science can the "experts" blame outsiders for the failure of their own predictions and still claim that their models are correct? Their models fail because they view economics as a natural speculative science instead of the practical science it really is.

Some will try and argue that this is not real science. They are wrong. Science is the discipline of applying the principles of reason to evidence in order to reach a conclusion about the cause of the evidence observed. The cause of economic activity is human nature; we have needs and desires. We are looking at evidence from the study human nature and the ultimate end for which human nature exists. We are examining particular economic actions and using the principles of reason to reach conclusions, not just about the monetary aspects of the transactions, but if they are consistent with human nature - will they help to fulfill that nature, or hinder that fulfillment. The conclusions are not based on the fads of the current time, but on more than 2,300 years of studying human nature.

Economics is not the science of money and how to get the greatest profit. It is the science of determining how people ought to act in transactional relationships in a way that is consistent with their true nature in order to fulfill their families' needs and wants.

The Nature and Roles of Government

"A community of a higher order should not interfere in the internal life of a community of a lower order, depriving the latter of its functions, but rather should support it in case of need and help to coordinate its activity with the activities of the rest of society, always with a view of the common good."
- Pope John Paul II

The principle is called subsidiarity, and it is a crucial element of distributism. When we speak of these orders of community, we are trying to define the very structure of society. The orders of community are the levels of the societal structure. These communities are things like the family, social communities, religious communities, work communities, and the different levels of government. The purpose of this article is not to try and define the proper function of each of these levels, it is to discuss the basis for determining what those functions are. There can be some variation based on culture and circumstances, but the principles are universal. How is society defined? Why do different orders of community exist within a society? Why does this matter when we are discussing economics?

The answer to that last question was actually addressed in the previous articles of this series about socialism and capitalism. The economic order of society exists to fulfill the needs and wants of the families within it. Government is necessarily involved in protecting that economic order by implementing laws consistent with it. The laws concerning economic matters in capitalist, Keynesian, and socialist societies are based on those economic views. The laws concerning economic matters in a distributist society would have to be consistent with the economic view of distributism. It is therefore necessary to understand the functions of the different orders of community within a society to understand when one is improperly usurping the function of another. Because government has a role in protecting the economic environment of a society, subsidiarity has implications on how that role is to be fulfilled in economic legislation. Understanding subsidiarity will help us to understand what types of economic laws are properly the jurisdiction of the different orders of community.

In the distributist view, the family is the fundamental community in any society. If you imagine the society as the different orders of community stacked on top of one another, the family would be at the bottom, not because it is beneath or of less importance than the other orders, but because it is the foundation and support of the others. It is the basic community which the others exist to serve.

23

In the distributist view, higher orders of communities in a society only exist to fulfill social needs that cannot be sufficiently met by the family. The same is true as you move up the the order of communities, each higher order only exists to fulfill needs that cannot be sufficiently met by the lower order. Because of this, even though the higher orders are necessarily over the lower ones, the scope of authority gets narrower as you move up the levels of these orders. In other words, if you were to picture these orders stacked one upon the other, they would look like a pyramid.

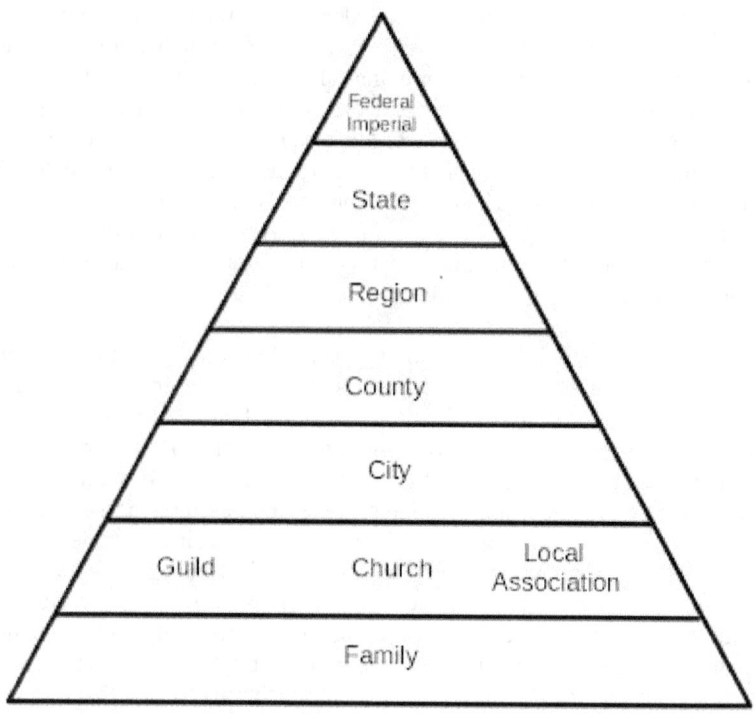

An important difference between subsidiarity and the view more commonly accepted in our society is that the higher levels don't get their authority from the lower levels. What authority they have is natural to them by their existence. This distinction is important because it is the basis for a true view of what some people call "limited government." Our society was founded on the idea that the lowest order (by which they mean individual citizens) grants power to the higher ones as part of some social contract. This is also the basis for believing they can also take power away from the higher order. The problem with this view is two-fold. First, it means that the people could potentially take away the authority a community of a higher order needs to fulfill its true function. Second, it means that lower orders can give what are naturally their own functions to the higher orders.

In the first case, you could potentially end up with a state that does not have the authority to provide national defense. I realize that this is not likely, but it is the logical conclusion of the position. Saying that higher levels of the social order get their authority from the lower levels means the authority can be revoked.

In the second case, you could end up with a state that has totalitarian powers simply because a majority of the people decided to give it that power. The state could end up with the power to decide what jobs you may have, how many children you may have, how those children must be educated and what they will be taught, what kind of car you may drive, and almost anything else. The state could have the power to take your children away from you simply because you believed something different than the majority. The state could even say that you must purchase something you don't want because it thinks that is best for society as a whole. This is also the logical conclusion of the position.

We live and interact in communities because that is our nature. If humans automatically and always acted with charity and justice toward each other, government wouldn't be necessary. However, because we don't do this automatically and always, we need a form of government in order to preserve the common good of the communities in which we live. This applies to all levels of community within a society, including the family. Parents govern the family for the common good of all its members. The point I'm trying to make here is that the authority of the government of each order of community is not granted to it from its members. Just as children do not establish the government of their parents or grant their authority, members of a higher order of community do not establish its government or grant its authority.

The government of a community exists by virtue of the community's existence, and its authority is over precisely those things which deal with preserving the common good of each member and the totality of its members in matters that go beyond their own authority. For example, because one family does not have a natural authority over another family, it cannot dictate on which side of the road cars should be driven, or how fast those cars should be allowed to drive in areas where children are commonly present and at play. However the common good requires that such rules exist because we must all act with due respect for the lives and safety of those children. The very act of living in community necessitates some form of government to deal with such matters.

This is not to say that the members of the higher order have no choice in their government. Even if the choice of leaders and the precise definition of laws involves the choice of its members, the existence and authority of a community's government is by its nature, by the needs it exists to fulfill to preserve the common good. Therefore, neither the higher, nor the lower, orders of community may usurp the roles and authorities that are part of the internal life of any given community. This applies regardless of the form of government. It applies equally to a monarchy, a republic, or any other form. Subsidiarity, therefore, takes an older view of the "social contract" idea, where the "contract" may establish the form of government and who will hold the positions of government, but is limited in terms of establishing the functions of government. It isn't simply a matter of "majority rule" or amending a constitution.

Our society is obsessed with the idea of rights. Unfortunately, the concept of "rights" has been warped almost to mean whatever people want to do. Rights in society are not granted by the government, nor are they granted by the city, or by groups of people protesting some perceived injustice. Rights are not based on people's desires, feelings, or wants. Rights are based on obligations which come from nature. There is no such thing as a right without an obligation to establish it. People think that freedom is achieved by protecting rights. In reality, freedom is achieved by protecting duties.

By having children, parents are obligated to care for, educate, and raise them to be virtuous people. They also become obligated to support and care for one another, for the common good of each other and the children they are obligated to raise. This is the basis of the idea of marriage as the establishment of a family, formally defining the obligations of its governing members toward each other and any children they may have. A higher order of society may provide schools to assist parents with the education of children, it could even establish guidelines for education, but it cannot force parents to use them if they want to seek another means to provide for that education. The attempt to do so would be interfering with the internal life of the family. Even though the city or state might be said to have a vested interest in the education of children, that interest is always secondary to that of the parents and family. Likewise, a city, by virtue of its establishment has the obligation to establish laws for the common good of those living in its jurisdiction. Even if the citizens of the city participate in determining what those laws should be, they do not have the authority to take that power away; it is a function and obligation of the city to establish and enforce those laws. It is only by acknowledging and protecting the inherent functions and duties of each order of community that true liberty can be established and protected in any society.

"... but rather should support it in case of need and help to coordinate its activity with the activities of the rest of society, always with a view of the common good."

There will be times when the lower orders of community need help. Families can suffer tragedy that leave them in need of assistance. Cities or larger regions can suffer situations, like natural disasters, that leave the inhabitants in need of assistance from other communities. These disasters can be wide-spread and simultaneously impact multiple communities. Higher orders of community exist to fulfill the needs that the lower orders cannot fulfill on their own. These are examples of cases where it is the duty of the higher orders (as well as other instances of the same or lower orders) to step in to support those in need. However, you need not envision disastrous scenarios to come up with examples. You can look at something as simple as driving on the roads. It is necessary for public safety (a common good) that upon crossing a city border a driver not be required to suddenly change the side of the road on which he must drive. This does not mean that the higher order must necessarily dictate which side shall be used. It could conceivably coordinate with the cities to reach an agreement which would then be binding on all. In the U.S., this is similar to how the old U.S. Route system worked. The states met together to agree on the routes and how they would connect. This system worked very well and established sufficient and reliable means of transportation from state to state and connected many small communities within each state.

People live in communities because that is human nature. By living in community, people have natural obligations toward one another. Each order of community exists for a purpose consistent with human nature to protect the common good for its members. This is the basic principle underlying subsidiarity at all levels. It isn't one rule for one class and another rule for another class. It is one rule for everyone. Subsidiarity is the basis for a true understanding of the idea of limited government. Subsidiarity is the firm basis for establishing protections for the freedom of individuals and the freedom of each order of community within a society. Subsidiarity is the foundation of true liberty.

Distributist Economic Society

In the introduction to this series, I stated that distributism is not a middle ground between capitalism on the one side and socialism on the other. Distributism is not an attempt to compromise between them. Instead, distributism stands outside of and completely apart from those systems. The goal of distributism is not to negotiate a common ground between the two, but to establish something completely different and alien to both.

There are two things that must be stated at the beginning of this last article in the series. First is the admission that capitalism could be accomplished in a just way. I affirm the fundamental right to private property and assert that, just as personal freedom is best guaranteed if it includes economic freedom, economic freedom is best guaranteed if the ownership of the majority of productive property in a society is distributed among as many of its citizens as possible. However, I must admit that a form of capitalism that accepted the fact that economics is a sub-field of an ethical system that recognized the primacy of people in society as a whole over personal monetary or material gain could be a just system. It has at least the potential to be one for which there would be few grounds for complaint. The main problem with capitalism is that the philosophical foundation behind it is essentially a utilitarian view which allows people to separate economics from ethics and can result in tremendous injustices for the common man.

Keynesian capitalism attempts to correct these injustices by giving greater authority to the government to help the poor at the expense of the wealthy while leaving as much as possible of the capitalist economic system in place. This has resulted in an increasingly totalitarian state which is "bought and sold" by the wealthy who use the power of government to further their own interests even more than the original capitalists. At the same time government establishes programs to help the poor, it also subsidizes big business and caters laws to the desires of big business even at the expense of the common man. In the end, Keynesian capitalism appears to be taking us on the road to either socialism or the Servile State described by Hilaire Belloc.

The second thing that must be said is that Socialism, despite its noble intent to alleviate the injustices working classes experienced under capitalism, inevitably creates an even more unjust society by denying the right to private ownership of productive property and by turning upside down the structure of political society, allowing the state to interfere with the inner workings of the lower orders of communities to the point of interfering with the very heart of society - the family. It inevitably establishes a totalitarian state and merely transfers the unjust economic power of the very wealthy into the hands of an already unjust state structure.

The basis for saying that distributism stands on one side and both capitalism and socialism on the other is that both capitalism and socialism consolidate the ownership and control of productive property into the hands of a small minority of the citizens. Although it must be admitted that capitalism does not *require* the consolidation of ownership of productive property, acceptance of that consolidation is necessary to accept capitalism because it is a natural result of what capitalists call free market competition. Some may argue that under socialism, ownership is not consolidated because it is owned by the people. However, without the ability to effectively direct and influence the use of productive property, you cannot say that you really have ownership. Therefore, the ownership of productive property under socialism is, realistically speaking, concentrated into the hands of the state officials. While, under socialism, those who control the overwhelming majority of economic power are the same as those who wield political power, the result of capitalism is that those who control the overwhelming majority of economic power use that power to exert control over those who wield political power.

The goal of distributism is to establish a greater distribution of both economic and political power. As I have stated elsewhere, this is not merely "a new plan." It is an entirely different philosophical view of the relationship between economics and the people and also between society and the people. Because of this, movement from the type of economic and political society we currently have to the distributist view will necessarily be gradual as (hopefully) more and more people accept that view. It will not start from the top of society, it will have to be from the people at the "grass roots" of society making changes on a personal level and then exerting pressure up the levels of society to adapt to what they want for the common good. This should be natural as the higher levels of society exist to serve the lower ones.

In the article on the roles and nature of government, I explained how authority in civil government is structured according to the principle of subsidiarity. That same principle applies to authority in a distributist economic society. The principle function of economics, which means "household management," is to provide for the needs of the family. Even though most economic activity appears to be only indirectly supporting the needs of the family, securing those needs is the fundamental basis without which there would be no economic activity. If you didn't need to secure food, you would not go out to buy it. If you didn't need to earn an income with which to buy the things you need and want from others, you would not need to work to earn that income. It does not matter if you are talking about international trade, interstate trade within a federation or empire, intrastate trade between regions or counties or other communities, or local trade with businesses within your own community, all economic activity ultimately takes place so that individuals can provide for the needs and wants of their families. It is important to keep this in mind, because it seems that many economists forget this very basic point and talk about economics and families as though they are only incidentally related.

Because of this, local orders of society need to have the most control over local economic matters. This is why distributists advocate the guild system with locally owned shops that are directly answerable to the local community. Higher orders of society should not be able to interfere in local economic matters to the extent they currently do. Take, for example, the Farm Bill in the United States. This is a collection of laws at the highest level of political society that directly interferes in local economic decisions. It subsidizes certain types of farm activity - keeping those prices artificially low - and makes alternate farming activity appear inefficient and expensive by comparison.

Why do you think locally grown organic products are more expensive? Why would it be more expensive *to not use* chemical fertilizers, antibiotics, processes like pasteurization and homogenization, patented genetically modified seeds, warehouse storage, and long distance shipping? Each of these things adds to the cost of production yet the products that use some or all of these things somehow cost less than those that don't. This is because the U.S. government not only subsidizes giant farms that use these processes, it and state governments routinely interfere with the small farms who don't - especially if they dare to offer something like raw dairy products. In a distributist society, federal, state, and even county governments would have less authority to interfere with local economic issues, leaving the majority of the authority with the citizens of the local community who live in and depend on that local economic environment. These are quite capable of devising health and safety standards.

This does not mean that higher levels of society have no involvement. The principle of subsidiarity does not require that. Instead, it provides the grounds for the local community to protect its own interests, thereby limiting the corrupting influence of big business on government policy. Higher levels of government can assist in times of need and even offer guidance, but without taking over.

Other practices that we now consider normal might also be changed to benefit the local economy. For example, zoning laws can be reconsidered so that it does not unnecessarily force people to commute. While it is reasonable for a community to decide that certain types of businesses should not be located near schools or places where people live, there are many types of businesses where I think this makes no sense. Why cannot a baker live in the same building, or at least on the same property, as his bakery? The notion that residential areas must be strictly separated from all business activities is one that not only creates more inconvenience for the local community, it forces a greater expense as prospective entrepreneurs must acquire two properties on which to live and work instead of just one. Eliminating this where practical would not only lower business costs, but it would also decrease traffic by placing many businesses where we work and where we shop within walking distance of home.

Distributism is economics as if families matter. It is economics as if local communities matter. It is economics that protects the small local business against the large one. It is economics that is not predatory. It is economics governed by ethics.

www.ingramcontent.com/pod-product-compliance
Lightning Source LLC
Chambersburg PA
CBHW070340190526
45169CB00005B/1983